Accelerated

Learning

Your Complete and Practical Guide to Learn Faster,
Improve Your Memory, and Save Your Time with
Beginners and Advanced Techniques

Table of Contents

INTRODUCTION: 5

CHAPTER 1: HOW WE LEARN   8

THE LEARNING PROCESS   9

THE CHANGING WORLD   17

THE FUTURE OF LEARNING   26

CHAPTER 2 – HOW MEMORIES WORK   33

SHORT-TERM MEMORY   36

LONG-TERM MEMORY   44

BAD MEMORY HABITS   52

CHAPTER 3 – IMPROVING MEMORY   58

BASIC TIPS   59

UNDERSTANDING VERSUS KNOWING   69

TENDING YOUR MEMORY   78

CHAPTER 4 – CONCENTRATION   86

FOCUSING ATTENTION   87

TAPPING INTO YOUR BRAIN   92

REDUCING STUDY TIMES   99

CHAPTER 5 – QUICK LEARNING TIPS   104

SWITCH IT UP   **105**

PRACTICAL TECHNIQUES   **112**

SPEEDY LEARNING   **119**

CHAPTER 6 – CHANGING MINDSET   124

THINKING CREATIVELY   **129**

THINKING ANALYTICALLY   **134**

TOOLS FOR CONTINUOUS LEARNING   **139**

CONCLUSION: 143

OTHER BOOKS BY TRAVIS O'RYAN   146

DID YOU ENJOY THIS BOOK?   **147**

INTRODUCTION:

Welcome to this training of accelerated learning for the Kindle. By purchasing this book, you have made the decision that you need a new method in which you will start to learn. This alone is all it takes to start to become more aware with a growth mindset that encourages change and aides in improving memory.

In our fast-paced world, not only is educational innovation present and available, but we also have a population that is demanding more. Every new invention we learn is just a stepping stone towards a greater innovation. Each new theory or discovery we make is just a chip away at a bigger truth that we're exploring.

With so much to be learned, we can't use the same old methods we have been for gaining new information. Instead, we have to make sure that we're keeping up with our methods of learning as quickly as we're keeping up with everything else that is so rapidly changing in the world.

Accelerated learning will help you not only process information faster, but also helps to make sure that you are improving your memory as well. The more we can expand our minds, the easier it becomes to actually grow them.

Throughout this book, you will first learn the science and processes of how we learn new things as well as how we store information. If you can understand the core of your brain, you can start to better understand everything else that comes along with it.

From there, we'll discuss the ways needed to improve memory as well as to increase your level of concentration. When this occurs, you'll be shocked at how much you can remember with little effort. The emphasis throughout the book will be on variation and practice. It's important to make sure that you keep switching things up. The only way to ever see an improvement in your mind and throughout the process will be to actually practice the techniques discussed.

We'll share plenty of examples for you throughout, so you can get a better understanding of the kind of things we'll be discussing. There will be tips and tricks for you to create your own learning plan so that you can implement the theories and ideas that work best for your pace and process for taking in new information.

CHAPTER 1: HOW WE LEARN

In order to improve what you learn and what you remember, you first have to understand how you do both of those things. The better you understand your brain in general, as well as a personal level, the more equipped you'll be with the tools necessary to increase your learning process.

Though it might feel like a newer experience for those that are in school, we have been learning since not long after our moment of conception. In order to figure out how you're learning now and what the best practices are for you to achieve a better understanding, we must start by looking at the way we learned as babies and kids.

THE LEARNING PROCESS

Learning is a scientific process. Though there might not be any chemistry, biology, or physics involved in the material you're learning, at the core, it's a process that involves all of those things happening in your brain. There are chemical reactions that are triggered by different things that you're learning. You should know by now, just as a person in general, that learning does not always occur in a classroom setting. Sometimes, just going to the grocery store can result in a huge life lesson that changes the course of your life. Or at the very least, your day.

It's clear that everyone learns differently, but why? If you have ten people in a room and you try to teach them all how to multiply, everyone will end up learning differently. Some people will understand right away, and others will take more time. Some people will learn better from reading off a chalkboard, and others will have to go home and think about it alone first before they actually grasp the concept.

Learning is dependent on how the neurons in your brain

send signals across synapses. Some people have larger parts of their brain than others, and some people are filled with chemicals that other people lack. Your brain is your own specific design based on genetics, past experiences, and current lifestyle. No two brains are alike, and if they were, they would still alter through time based on the things that we allow into our lives.

Learning is dependent on things that you already know. It might seem obvious, but sometimes we can forget that. You learn by taking the new information and applying it to the things that you already know. You also can only understand so much based on the concepts that you already comprehend. That is why, the more you know, the faster you will be able to learn new concepts. Those that already know two languages will be able to learn a third language faster than those that only speak in their native tongue.

As Babies and Kids

We start learning as early as in the womb. Before you even have the chance to open your eyes or take your first breath after birth, you are starting to develop your skills and all the different chemicals in your brain. What your biological mother does (unless born via surrogacy), what she eats, and what she exposes herself to, all determine certain levels of your learning as you grow inside of her body.

Patterns and repetition are ways that babies learn as well. Once you are born, you start identifying different patterns that help you learn about the things around you. Before you can speak, read, or write, you will know that when you see your mother, father, or another caretaker, that this person is the one responsible for making sure you don't cry, or feeding and changing you. This is because when you start crying, their face appears.

Surprise, for both infants and children, is a way that they learn new things as well. Though it can seem like little kids are more interested in repetition (who has not played hide and seek with a child that hides in the same spot every time?), it is the surprise of new things that help them learn the most. For example, if they are playing with a red ball over and over again, and a blue ball gets introduced, they will give that more attention, as they have become used to the old ball. This simple kind of thinking is important to carry throughout the rest of the book. New information is the way to accelerate learning.

Kids do have limits on what can be learned. A child's brain can only go so far, but just with their level of comprehension and not the actual amount that they can know. All brains are limitless, but it takes a few more steps than just reading or watching something to actually start learning and comprehending different ideas.

Through Education

Problem-solving is a natural motivator. Kids have this instinctive urge to find solutions to different things without even being initially prompted. Problem-solving is the way that many children are introduced to new ideas. Addition is the first thing we learn in math, besides what numbers are, of course. Most of the time, this will be exemplified by saying things like, "Jimmy has five apples and then buys two. How many apples does he have now?" Though counting apples is not a problem that 5 or 6-year olds have, it is still the method in which they will learn different things.

Children also seek their own challenges. If you give a child a puzzle, they will try to figure it out without being told to do so in the first place. It's a natural instinct for humans to investigate an issue and try to determine the best solution to a problem.

Practicing is the greatest tool for children to learn. It's the only method that works for positive cognitive growth. Children are hands-on, and they like being involved. The idea of being needed carries with us throughout our entire lives, but children feel this need for purpose as well. When they're given the proper tools for practice and application, they will thrive.

Children do not have the capabilities to just memorize things. They will certainly be able to remember a lot, but they will not grasp this information unless they are given a practical way to apply that knowledge. This is true for some adults as well, but more teens and older individuals can memorize something and understand it without actually having to apply it to their real life.

In the World

In some cases, we no longer seek new information when we become adults. High school or college graduation might be the last time someone actually sits in a room to learn new concepts and ideas. Though we no longer expose ourselves to teaching methods, this does not mean we are not still learning. In fact, many of us learn more after we're out of school than we ever did while we were in school.

This is because of the constant need to apply concepts. Just think of it in terms of money. You took several math classes throughout high school and college, understanding that one plus one equals two. As an adult, when you first started out with money, you still probably had a period in your life where you had to figure out a budget. Though you were very aware that you made

$300 and were spending $350, you still likely had to go through trial and error phases to figure out what budget works best, even though you had a good understanding of basic mathematics that you gained in your education. This is because knowledge does not always mean anything unless you actually apply it to real life scenarios.

As we navigate through our adult lives, we tend to put a focus on only relevant information. Sometimes this is good, other times, it's bad. For example, maybe you really enjoy jazz music. You will then continually learn about new jazz artists and shows through the radio, internet, and other friends that share interests. This is great, as you're growing your knowledge in this subject. However, you might be completely overlooking other popular music categories, putting all your focus on just jazz. This is fine when it comes to personal taste and the things you like. However, this method of seeking only relevant information can be harmful when we only look at one news source for political information or only choose one theory when trying to explore different parts of our life.

The reason why you might find yourself maturing so much faster as you leave your parent's homes is because of the forced practical-ism of new ideas into the real world. For this reason, it is clear that the method to accelerate learning is a hands-on approach that requires practical application. Though it is much easier to just sit down and read about how to sail rather than actually taking sailing lessons, in the end, a person who practically applied these skills is going to be much better off. Part of this is because of trial and error. There is no chance to make a mistake when you are reading in the comfort of your own home. Sometimes, the most valuable information simply comes from the mistakes that we have made.

If we don't practice learning, we run the risk of losing that essential tool that we were granted from birth. You can sit in your house all day, watch jeopardy, read encyclopedias, and trivia books, but are you really smarter than someone that is traveling the world and continually gaining new experiences? Maybe, but you really have to look at both experiences on an individual level to determine the way they learn and how much information they are taking in as well.

THE CHANGING WORLD

Kids care more about understanding practical information than they did before. Studies have shown that kids place more of an emphasis on globalization and understanding the world around them than they do by applying different math or science. With the technology we have at our fingertips, we no longer need to remember different "facts." You don't need to understand how to multiply, as you can do so with your calculator. It's not that it's irrelevant or unimportant, it's just that you can survive in the real world now with different information required than all the things that our parents had to know.

You have to look at what is available and understand how this can be applied in our changing world. Instead of just trying to remember information, there is more of an emphasis now on actually grasping those concepts and having comprehension of different theories and methods that work. Human beings might seem like the most aware creatures on the planet, but we still have a lot more room to work with awareness in order to achieve a good level of being self-aware. Our technology seems to put more of an emphasis on this awareness in making sure that we understand who we are, what we're made of, and how that actually affects the planet in which we live.

There's quicker exposure to new information than there was just a decade ago. News stories could be dragged out for months at a time when really, no new information was given on any particular subject. Nowadays, people are hungry for a new story every hour. Instead of watching the news for three hours in the morning, young adults would rather just check their social media to see what relevant stories their friends might have been sharing. Whether or not you believe this is a good or bad thing is subjective, but it is true that we're no longer satisfied with a slower rate of the release of information.

Observing how the changing world affects learning is important, but we also need to understand that we have to find new ways of learning in order to keep up with the world. There are some things that work in applications and methods from decades ago that still hold relevancy to learning now. To try and pretend like we shouldn't continually grow our teaching and learning methods is ignorant.

Demand for Speed

The things around us change faster than we're even able to change different outfits. Before the morning, you can guarantee there will be a new meme or viral story that everyone online is talking about. It used to take years for some information to catch on, but now, things change faster than our bowel movements. Celebrities pop up overnight, living out their fifteen minutes of fame, then dissolving once the new meme star comes along. We have been spoiled with the speed at which we are given new information, and now that we have seen that side of the world, there is no going back to the old ways.

The way we consume different materials demands speed as well. Just look at the popularization of quick social media sharing. Vine required users to tell a story within a few seconds, and Snapchat and Instagram introduced similar features as well. Eventually, Facebook caught on, and who knows how many other platforms will appear that allow people to tell entire cinematic stories within a matter of seconds. Though films are still important, and many people spend a large part of their time binge-watching hour-long shows, we still have the demand to get information as fast as possible. Some people don't want to sit and read a cookbook anymore. They would rather just watch a ten-second video of someone else using an Instant Pot. In some ways, this is better. Instead of having to buy the cookbook, buy the ingredients, and figure out how to craft the meal, you can watch someone else do it for you, knowing whether or not you will actually want to eat the meal after it has been cooked. There are still negative sides to this, with many people unable to sit and concentrate for more than a few minutes at a time because they have trained their brain to only accept quick information.

Children's brains are developing faster than ever before as well. Studies have proven that children can take in information from two sources at once, comprehending both concepts as well. You have probably found yourself sitting on your phone in front of the TV, and maybe you even had your laptop and a tablet open in front of you. These four different devices are simultaneously giving you new information, but you might not always keep up with them. Younger children are able to take in the same amount of information from two different sources without having to split their attention. That is huge! Just imagine what our children's children will be capable of. With this rapid ability to learn new things, it's clear that there is a huge change coming in our education system.

We have to be accommodating to this huge change. It's easier to just stick to what we already know, but it's clear that the world is demanding change. Though these methods have proven to work for generations, we still have to continue to improve upon the way we teach and learn to optimize the amount of information we are getting. The faster we learn, the faster we can change the world for the better.

Using Technology

Technology is not meant to be scary. There are science

fiction novels and horror movies about technology taking over. The thing that we must remember, however, is that technology does not have intention. It only does what it's programmed to do. If a robot is programmed to kill, it will do this. However, that robot was only told to do so by the person that created it in the first place. Whenever you feel scared of technology, remind yourself it is the humans that are in control that you actually have to be fearful of.

Technology allows for some people to consume more than one thing at once. You can listen to an audiobook while also watching someone build a house on YouTube. How much you are able to take in from both of these sources is dependent on you alone, but it's still crazy to think about how much we are actually able to take in at once.

We must also consider how technology can be used to help those that might not be as quick of learners as others. Technology helps children with learning disabilities find a specialized program to suit their needs. A few decades ago, any child with a disability was lumped into one group and sent to a different classroom, assuming that just because they weren't "normal," they were alike in the way they think. Children with Downs Syndrome, ADHD, Asperger's, and Autism all think in different ways, so instead of just categorizing them into a "special needs" room, we can make sure that they are getting the individual treatment they need because of different technological advances, and the use of AI as an actual teacher.

Technology must be implemented into the future of learning, but we can't always be dependent upon this tool alone. While we'd be foolish to overlook the accommodation required by technology, we can't also forget that the key to accelerated learning still lies within our brain.

Continual Growth

Have you ever heard someone say that they haven't read a book since high school? As if this is something to be proud of. It's true that once you graduate high school or college, most people can navigate through their life without having to read a single thing other than a traffic sign or a menu. While you will not die if you don't read a book, does that mean you will actually live a fulfilling life? The key to accelerated learning is constantly improving your mind and increasing how much, and what, you know. If you just stick to the ideas you already have, never expanding upon them, your brain remains stagnant.

Think of it like exercise. Once you lost that hundred pounds, it'll come back if you don't keep up with it. It took a while to gain the weight, it'll take a while to get rid of it. Once you reach your goal weight, you have to at least maintain a certain level of exercise to make sure that it doesn't come back. If your goal is to live a fulfilled life, you have to make sure that you maintain a mindset in which you are constantly expanding on your thoughts and learning new things.

Continual growth helps us improve our skills, no matter what area they might be in. If you work in the medical field, you probably know that you must attend certain conferences or meetings to renew and keep your license or certification. You might sit behind a desk and file paperwork all day, but that doesn't mean you shouldn't keep up with new information and advancing technologies in order to maintain the skills you' worked so hard to achieve while in medical school.

The more you know, the more you realize that you do not know. If you learn a new word, you will learn about all the different words that come along with that, and the way that you can apply that meaning. If you discover a new country, you'll realize that you still have to learn about all the cities and towns within that country too. Anyone who believes they "know it all," more than likely does not know anything. The key to being an intelligent person is realizing that you might not be that intelligent after all. You will at least realize that there is so much more to know while accepting that there might be some things you never know anything about.

THE FUTURE OF LEARNING

Some people fear the future of learning. They wonder if technology will take all of the human jobs available and if one day, we might not need to have teachers at all. As we already discussed, a robot is not going to do anything unless it is told to. We still know little about AI and how to create it, but maybe one day we will make a conscious robot that knows how to harvest bodies Matrix style. When that day comes, we can worry, but at the moment, it's challenging to make a phone that knows the difference between "duck," and another curse word.

Learning will never go away, but it's certainly going to change. Some people fear that since we can Google anything we need to know within seconds, we're not going to learn anything new anymore. That is one perspective, but it's not the truth. In reality, we might not need to know how to apply a mathematical formula since we have a calculator with us, but that only means that we have freed up the time to explore new mathematical practices.

The goal for learning should be continual growth. What

is the point of knowing anything if you don't care about discovering more? With technology at our fingertips, we have created a world that allows anyone, no matter if they have a disability, or if they are financially strapped for cash, to continually learn something new. Right now, if you really wanted to, for whatever reason, you could open up your phone and learn the basics of rocket science. A few decades ago, you'd have had to go to a library, maybe even get an interview with a rocket scientist to understand the basic knowledge behind this subject. Now, there is probably a listicle, or likely even a few to choose from, titled, "10 Things You Didn't Know About Rocket Science."

We should be hopeful and excited about all the potential for learning developments as time goes on. As our brains grow, so does our world. Centuries ago, people only live into their twenties. Now, we have people that have come close to reaching their 120's! Though elongating life is not always the goal, there are still other ways in which science will seriously improve our overall quality of life. We just have to be ready and willing to take in all this new information.

There will be more of a personalized focus on learning, allowing for a better education overall on a diverse level. The reason why some people might fall so behind in school is because they can't keep up with other people. This is not because they are stupid, they just learn in a different way. That same person that fell behind could have become a doctor responsible for saving lives, but instead, they choose a different career path because they couldn't keep up in their third-grade science class. With more personalized and individual learning experiences, children will have the ability to learn at the same level without getting discouraged or forced into a pace that sets them up for failure.

Picking What to Remember

As education changes, there will be a more personalized approach where children can choose what to learn. This means that if a child enjoys science more than history, they can choose to put their attention towards that, growing a strong scientific brain from an early age.

It's still important to incorporate all subjects, as

everything in this world is connected on some level. How many people wanted to be a certain profession when they were five, only to realize they have no interest in that career path whatsoever now?

Children will also have the ability to lead their classroom. There are many intelligent people in the world, but the education system is not always created to where everyone has access to better learning and mindful development. If a child can choose their own curriculum, they are more likely to pay attention to the things they are learning instead of falling behind, setting the course for the rest of their lives.

Research on Learning

There is more focus done on how video games affect a children's ability to learn. Video games that have fearful moments and scary scenes actually set certain children up with ways of facing their fears. Simulation games allow people to live out experiences they might not be able to otherwise, all while developing cognitive skills. Video games get some heat because of their level of violence, but we have to remember that this is just one genre.

The brain is a complex organ that still has yet to be explored. We can figure out a lot from what we know, but as brain research develops, so will everything else. The more we discover, the more we will realize how many other things we have to discover. For example, imagine a scenario in which a new species is discovered.

This might have been done by a new use of technology, and the species might be one that is endangered that we can help protect. However, once we discover that species, we have also discovered the fact that we have to learn everything about it. The diet, lifespan, habitat, and other basic understandings of the subject all have to be explored once a new creature is discovered, proving the more we know, the more we have to learn.

Learning how we learn can sound complicated, but it's important to make sure that we know what it takes to continue to teach our kids in a way that is better than how *we* learned. While it's important to continually analyze and decide what information is important to teach and what isn't relevant, we also have to consistently analyze how certain things are being taught.

Experience Versus Lecture

Experience is always a better learning tool than actually sitting down and memorizing information. It's easier to just read a book, but it's not going to be the actual way to understand a concept. Practical application is and will always be the best method of learning.

You will hear many people describe themselves as visual learners, but not many other people say that they learn best by being in a quiet room alone and not talking to anyone else while they memorize words from a book. Most people are visual learners because we have been designed that way. The best method of remembering something is by using all five of your senses and having a physical experience to associate with that. This is because our brain takes in information all day.

The color of the walls that surround you, what you're wearing, what mood you are in, and what makes up the person sitting closest to you is all information your brain takes in. It has to filter all of these things, deciding what is relevant and what is not to hold onto. Our brains are much more likely to put information in a secured and safe storage spot in our brain if we actually take the time to learn something through an applicatory process.

If you attended a large university, you likely understand the importance of practical application rather than just knowledge. Think back to any lecture you might have had in a huge hall that held hundreds of students. It was likely a class at a 100 level that didn't require as much knowledge. As you advanced into the 300 and 400 level classes, the size got smaller and eventually, you might have ended up in an internship where you worked one on one. This is because the best method of learning is to get hands-on in a situation working.

Applying experience is more personalized, so it's easier to find relevancy. You will discover throughout the rest of the book just how important it is to put an emphasis on experience and not just trying to memorize something. Having a solid memory is crucial in learning, but there is a difference between just memorizing and understanding new information. Before we get into more practical accelerated learning and memory improving techniques, we're going to look at one more chapter of how our brains work on a fundamental level.

CHAPTER 2 – HOW MEMORIES WORK

Our mind is incredibly complex, and even those that are skilled in brain study might have trouble understanding why we do certain things, and what parts of our brains are responsible for which activities. You might never fully understand your brain and why it operates the way it does, but you can start to look at how you process information and what turns into a memory. When you have an understanding of these basic ideas, you'll be able to better create a plan for improving your own memory.

Sensory Storage

The nervous system is responsible for learning. This involves taking in information about different senses. Everything you touch signals a response to your brain. From there, your brain will tell you if that item was hot, cold, soft, rough, metal, fabric, or anything else you need to know about a certain area you touch. When you smell or hear something, you are sending signals to your brain about what makes up these sources of sensory information. Seeing and tasting do the same thing. If any part of your brain responsible for a certain sense is not functioning properly, you will not get the same read on a specific sense.

This is a raw reaction to something that we will eventually learn. Any pain or pleasure from a certain sense that you experience lets your brain know information about the reaction to that sensory experience. We remember the feelings of pleasure so that we continue to do things that are good for us. You might become less sensitive to certain pleasure, but it will always remain there. If you don't overload that sense and go back to it at a later time, you will feel that same initial reaction.

The same is said about pain. Your body stores pain so that you do not do it again. Your body remembers pain, but it doesn't remember the sensory feeling so that if it happens again, you still have the initial reaction to trigger a better habit. For example, if you are hungry, you might get a stomach ache. Next time you are hungry, you will remember that stomach ache so that you eat. You won't, however, get used to the pain of a stomach ache because your body knows that if it stores this feeling of pain, you might never eat again because you do not feel that initial pain reaction.

Let's use an example of someone touching a hot pan straight out of the oven. There is a good chance that as a child, you were told not to touch hot things. You didn't know why, but you just knew that it was not a good idea to put your finger on a pot, pan, or another hot item that your parental figure was using to cook with.

So, let's say that you decided one day you were going to figure out what all the fuss was about. You touch the pot, and right away, your body tells you that it's hot. Before you even realize that, hey, mom was right after all, or that you're going to have a nasty blister popping up on your hand soon, your first thought was "ow!"

After that initial sensory reaction was experienced, that memory moves throughout your brain from your short-term to your long-term memory.

SHORT-TERM MEMORY

Most people can store between five and nine things in their short-term memory. Your short-term memory includes the small things that carry you throughout your day. The five things in your current short-term memory might include the words you are reading in this book, the fact that you have to call your doctor and make an appointment, what you are going to eat next, and any other tasks that are relevant to the next ten minutes or so of your life.

Your short-term memory includes holding onto information that is necessary to carry out a certain task. Your short-term memory holds onto all the little things you are thinking about in any given moment. This includes numbers such as a phone number you have to call or the weather that you just checked. It might include small things you have to do on a to-do list, like take out the garbage. Your short-term memory is also as simple as the feeling that you have to urinate, or a stomach grumble letting you know that it's time to eat.

Reading this book right now is using your short-term

memory. All of the information that your brain takes in which includes anything that passes through your sensory storage, then it goes into your short-term memory. What your senses feel is your initial reaction, and now that it's in your short-term memory, it's time to start processing these reactions to determine their purpose, use, intention, and meaning.

The brain does not do its "fleshing out" in short-term memory. Think of your short-term memory like the security check before getting onto the plane. Do you let that item through, or do you send it back out into the world?

Prefrontal Cortex

Your prefrontal cortex is the part of your brain responsible for short-term memory. This is why someone that has brain damage to the front of their heads might have difficulty with short-term memory. It's not that you don't remember things you recently learned, rather, you just don't hold onto any new information that is given. A person with a damaged prefrontal cortex might not be able to learn anyone's name unless they're told hundreds of times throughout months, and even then, they might still have completely lost the ability to remember a person's name at all.

The visual cortex might be activated in this part of your brain. This is responsible for creating images in order to help you understand different things. This is where instant association might start. If you see a sign for McDonald's while driving down the street, your prefrontal cortex kicks on and makes you think, "Hm, I'm kind of hungry and should maybe stop for a Big Mac."

Broca's area is responsible for repetition in learning. When you learn a new phone number, you might repeat it over and over to yourself in order to make it stamp into your memory. If you learn a new song, you're going to play it again so that you can understand and learn all of the new words. Each different part of your brain has a different responsibility, so if you discover that a certain part is not functioning, you can target that area to determine the best course of action.

Our brain keeps this all separated as sort of a survival technique. If we took in everything at once, immediately storing it in the same way, we would overload our senses and become confused. Taking memories in at a sensory level, processing them in the prefrontal cortex, and then sending them to other parts of the brain is just our way of processing things. This allows us to react properly and come up with solutions that help improve and grow our life overall.

Short-Term Storage

The reason we have this sort of filter is because we don't always need to remember everything that we take in. If you're watching a commercial or just listening to a random song on the radio, your mind reacts, but it knows on some level that it doesn't have to take all of this information in. When you are meeting someone new, you might not remember their name if you do not think it is all that important. What you decide to keep in your short-term storage can tell you more about yourself than you might have initially realized.

A technique to help grow your short-term memory is to make sure that you decide right when you learn something, whether or not you need to keep that information around. For example, if you meet a new important person, such as your boss's boss, when they say, "Hello, I'm Rachel," you might tell your brain, "remember her name is Rachel." By telling yourself right away that you need to remember something. Your brain will send a signal to your long-term memory, helping out to make sure that you keep this information stored rather than letting it get wasted.

Your short-term memory only exists for a few moments. By the end of the day, the things you learned from the morning have either become memories or have been disposed from your brain altogether. You never fully forget things. Your brain is not like a stomach that poops the actual waste out. It just won't become a solid memory. For example, let's pretend that your occupation is a waiter or waitress. Maybe you worked the breakfast shift and had a busy morning. Then, when you are finally in bed at the end of the day, you suddenly realize that you forgot to get the old man at table 6 the water that he asked for. This is because this memory never made it into your long-term memory.

The reason why you might forget some important things is because you just let it slip through your short-term storage and didn't put an emphasis on sending it to the long-term part. Once we start to become aware of how our memories work and the functions involved in teaching the brain what to remember and what to forget, we can improve the things we hold onto better.

Improving Synapses

Synaptogenesis is a process in which your brain forms new synapses. This is a rapid process during childhood and certainly slows once you reach adult years. This process promotes neural flexibility. By learning new information, you're ensuring that your level of synaptogenesis is continually strengthening. Even if you are a very intelligent person that graduated medical school, this process will slow once you graduate. You have to make sure that you are keeping up with new information in order to promote this process.

43

All the mind-altering drugs you have taken, any alcohol digested, or even just binging pointless YouTube videos all day have all caused certain brain synapses to become weak. Even though our brain is a sensitive organ that can be easily damaged, we still have the chance to improve these synapses and strengthen them. Do not assume anyone that takes recreational drugs or drinks alcohol is a dumb person because of this either. You do not kill all your synapses from smoking marijuana or drinking alcohol a few times here and there. If you smoke multiple times a day and drink heavily on a daily basis, there's certainly a higher chance that you have killed off some of your brain cells. In the same breath, if you do these things in a healthy way and only socially enjoy your alcoholic beverages or indulge in a glass of wine for dinner, you could actually be promoting synapse improvement. If you allow yourself to be too stressed out, you are not doing your brain any favors either, so indulging in something mind-numbing to take the edge off will do more good than harm.

Exercise is a great way to improve your synapses. This does not mean you have to get to the gym and lift weights for hours a day. Get up and walk around. Get the blood flowing back to your brain. When you are studying, and you just feel like you are not learning anything anymore, stand up and stretch. Give yourself at least twenty minutes of time to be physical each day. This is not with the intention of losing weight or sticking to a fitness routine. You just have to make sure you are dedicating some time to sending a good amount of blood back to your brain, so it can continue functioning properly. A good method to incorporate short exercise in your day is to stretch when you wake up, before you go to bed, or before your shower. We all have at least ten minutes here and there to devote to moving our arms and legs in order to help increase overall brain function.

LONG-TERM MEMORY

Your long-term memory is unlimited. You can read every book ever written, watch every movie ever made, and listen to every song ever sung, and you will still have more room leftover in your brain for new information. There is not a single number of things you can learn. Your head will not get bigger, but your world certainly will.

Accessibility is the problem with retrieving information from your long-term memory, not your availability. You could read a hundred books in a year, but if you didn't spend any time making sure that you improved your memory and cognitive function, you might not be able to recall anything that you read. It is not about what's stored in your brain, but how you are able to access it. If you store a certain memory from childhood, there's a good chance you might not have fully comprehended that situation because you become aware of it as a child. For example, maybe you witnessed something horrible, like your father hitting your mother. As a child, you didn't know why this was happening. These were your two caregivers, so you might even expect this to be normal behavior. Then, as you get older, you learned to push that memory down so deep in your long-term memory that you forget it. Then, it comes back to you one day when you witness a similar scene in a movie. You weren't able to tap into that memory because you didn't understand how to access it, not that it wasn't available.

You do not always get to choose what becomes a long-term memory. That is why you might easily remember the jingle to a soap commercial for a product that you have never even used, but not be able to remember your first day of kindergarten. Your brain was working while you weren't to store that repetition in your brain, but as a kindergartner, you didn't realize the importance of your first day of school, so that whole memory was never stored. Now that you're an intelligent adult that is seeking education, you'll be able to better choose what makes it to the long-term and what can be left in the short-term.

There are many different parts of our brains involved in the storage of memory, and there are variations of the types of long-term memories as well. For example, your hippocampus, perihelial and entorhinal cortexes all help to process information and either dump things or send them to your long-term memories. Some people's hippocampi might be stronger than others, and the same goes with other parts. This is why you might be great at remembering people's names and lousy at remembering how to properly cook a meal. Then, you might have a friend who's a wizard in the kitchen, but she has trouble remembering her own name. You both are good at remembering things, but it involves different aspects of your conscious, unconscious, and remote memories.

Unconscious Memory

Your unconscious memory might also be referred to as your implicit memory. This is all the stuff that gets stocked into your brain without you being consciously aware that it is even happening. This might be exemplified by a time when you pulled into your driveway after a long day at work, not even remembering that you had actually driven all the way home. You'd driven that path a thousand times before, so you didn't even need to become conscious of that memory in order to make it again.

You are not always aware of everything involved in your implicit memory. Random song lyrics, how to pour a bowl of cereal, and even how to wipe your butt are all unconscious memories that you do not think of as learning processes on a daily basis. These are things so natural to you that you could do them in your sleep, and your brain has been conditioned to follow through with these activities with little effort. This is why you might go through the motions of an action without even realizing exactly what you're doing.

Part of your unconscious memory involves procedural memory. This is inclusive of your motor skills, and the habits that come naturally to you. Not only is the act of brushing your teeth natural to you but deciding to do this might be natural as well. Most of us don't forget to brush our teeth unless we completely forgot a toothbrush or are in an environment different than what we're used to. You might wake up day after day, go pee right away, and then brush your teeth. These are all different motions that you do not even second guess.

Your unconscious memory is knowing "how." Every time you take a shower, you might pick up the soap and start rubbing it on your body. You are not thinking about this process. It comes naturally to you. If we didn't go through these motions naturally sometimes, our brains might be overloaded. If every morning, you had to relearn how to go pee and brush your teeth, you'd be exhausted before you could even get dressed.

Remote Memory

Remote memory involves a recollection of things that happened years ago. Our remote memory is another tricky part of our brain that we have little control over. Isn't it funny how you might have a lasting memory that you didn't even realize was significant at the time it occurred? Maybe it was a small conversation with your friend after midnight when you were both sleepy and delusional. Maybe it was a quick chat with someone in line at the bank, or perhaps it was just the memory of lying next to someone you love in bed. There are certain memories that we try to make stand out in our brain, like our first kiss, weddings, the day we graduate, and baby showers. These days will play important roles in our life, but there are other, deeper memories that play just as important roles. We do not always get to decide what stands out and what is forgotten.

Remote memory is what people might typically refer to as long-term memory, though it is just a way to define specific memories. Your long-term memory is pretty much everything you know, but your remote memory is specifically things that have happened months ago or longer.

What you had for breakfast is in your long-term memory, but what you had for breakfast last year is in your remote memory. You might think of remote memory as the last step in your memory process, but that isn't true either. You could hold onto one ten-minute-moment for your entire life in your remote memory, even if you go decades without thinking of that specific time.

Conscious Memory

Your conscious memory includes facts and bits of

information that you recall continually. This is how to carry out the tasks at your job, the name of your favorite TV show, and the dates of when your bills are due. Your conscious memory is the information that you are aware of and that you address. Your conscious memory is when you go over what you have to do during the day while you are brushing your teeth or taking your morning shower.

Your unconscious memory refers to the "how," and your conscious memory refers to the "what." You consciously decide what you're going to eat for breakfast, and then your unconscious memory pours the cereal. Your conscious memory is pretty much the only thing that shuts off in your brain at any given time. This is because it is working the hardest and needs its rest. When your conscious memory is silenced, then your remote memory and unconscious memory become relevant, which is why you have dreams or even daydreams. Your conscious mind needs a break, but since your brain can never shut off without you dying, your unconscious memory will take over.

Amnesia and other forms of memory loss involve losing parts of your conscious memory. This is why a coma patient that just woke up does not remember their family member's names, but they do not question what it means to be a person. We often expect those with amnesia, in movies or other forms of media at least, to wake up and question where they are in terms of the planet in general. If you lost your memory, you'd assume you'd wake up in a body and start freaking out, asking questions about the Earth and how it functions. This is not the case. You will simply lose your conscious memory and the things that it takes to remind you of your identifying factors and the things that make you an individual. You will still have most of your unconscious memories that are required for basic everyday functions. How far back these memories go are dependent upon the level of injury that has been suffered.

If you're suffering memory loss, you're not going to poop your pants because going to the bathroom is a skill you learned as a child and it has been stored as part of your long-term memory. Where the bathroom is, however, might be something you forget if you're in a newer or unfamiliar environment. If the memory loss is serious, you might have to go through the basic motions of learning these things again, which is why some stroke victims have to go through therapy to learn how to walk or talk again.

BAD MEMORY HABITS

Some people might just have a better way to remember certain things, and you might think this is just biologically genetic. You might see the smartest person in your class and think, man, I wish I could just learn like they do. The thing is, you can! They just have different lifestyles, memories, and genetic makeups that might have made it easier for them to be the good rememberer they are, but all our brains are capable of having the same functions.

It is true that there is biology involved in memory, but that doesn't mean that you can't still change your current state. If you have a family history of forgetfulness, you are more susceptible for sure, but that doesn't mean you are incapable of remembering things. It is all dependent on internal and external factors that affect your cognitive function overall.

There are ways of improving memory, and it is important to understand this, so you can continue to live a happy and healthy life. Forgetting things is not only just inconvenient, but it can be frustrating. No one wants to have to question their own brain. It is the only one we got, so we have to make sure we're doing our best to take care of it. The next three sections will go over the three major reasons you might have poor memory aside from just not properly learning information that needs to be remembered.

Diet

Toxins in your body lead to inflammation, which is why many people might suffer from a bad memory. Toxins can be found in unhealthy food, as well as any recreational drugs or alcohol. If we consume too many of these to the point where our body starts storing them during digestion rather than expelling them from our body, it will show in our overall cognitive performance.

Various refined sugars can lead to the build-up of plaque in a brain, which will thus lead to a lower cognitive function. Inflammation of the brain is the biggest reason why someone has trouble learning or remembering certain information. Inflammation is not inherently bad. It is your body's reaction to an outside threat. If you get a cut on your arm, it is likely the skin around the cut becomes puffy and red. This happens in order to make sure that the cut doesn't become infected. When you are putting toxins into your body, it will inflame in a similar way as your skin. While this might seem good, it can end up decreasing brain function and stopping necessary hormones that aid in learning and memorization.

Foods like leafy greens, dark-skinned fruits, and even some fatty oils help improve brain function. Anything that has anti-inflammatory properties is a great source in order to combat any feeling of memory loss or lower brain function.

Not all of the tastiest food is bad for memory. Chocolate and coffee can help increase memory function, but it is important to choose the right kind. Refined sugars found in junk food and starchy foods is the biggest culprit of inflammation. If you do choose to drink coffee, limit how much sugar or sweetener you add, and dark chocolate is always a better choice as opposed to milk chocolate that might include negative fatty acids.

Sleep

You actually help develop and solidify your thoughts during sleep. You have shut your conscious memory off momentarily which means your unconscious mind gets the chance to work out the information, worries, and hopes that have all passed through your brain on any given day.

The purpose of dreams is still unknown, but there are some theories that suggest it is your brains "dumping" process. You constantly load up your brain with new bits of information all day every day. Even though you might have spent your Sunday cuddled up on the couch binge-watching a show that you have already seen twice, you still have given your brain some new knowledge it needs to process. While you sleep, your brain cycles through this new info, as well as the remote memories you already have, to help determine what might be important and what might be useless.

If you do not get enough sleep, you are not giving your brain the rest it needs to fully function. It is just like any other part of your body. If you work it too hard, it' not going to perform at its highest capabilities.

It is also been discovered that we actually clean out more toxins when we are sleeping as well. Why this happens is not specifically known, but sleep will help reduce inflammation as your body will not be as focused on fighting off different toxins that you allow into your body.

Stress

Stress is inescapable. No matter who you are, you still likely feel stress at one point during your day, at the very minimum. Some of us are stressed out from the moment we wake up to the moment we go to bed. Stress is not completely invalid or lacking value. Benefits of stress include the preparation for certain scenarios, remembering mistakes so they do not get repeated, and a realization of the feelings and emotions in which you wish to solidify.

Though there are some benefits, stress is still damaging to your brain. When you are feeling stressed out, various hormones are released, causing changes in your brain that will affect memory. The more stressed out you are, the more damage that is done to the brain. Do not start stressing about being stressed, as this just makes things worse. Just remember that if you are stressed, it is likely not doing you any good.

Your body focuses on releasing a chemical called cortisol when you are stressed. An excess of cortisol actually blocks your hippocampus from functioning properly, causing a delay in memory. Aside from affecting the internal workings of your brain, stress is a distraction. If you allow yourself to be too stressed, you will miss out on what's happening around you, not allowing yourself to solidify a memory and choose to store it in a place in your head that you can later access.

Stress also causes physical effects on your body, which will end up taking more energy from the brain as well. Glucose is sent to different surrounding muscles when you are stressed, which will mean your brain is not getting enough of the food that it needs to properly function. Next time you are feeling stressed, remember to check how it might be causing you to physically hold your body. There's a good chance that either your shoulders, fists, or jaw will be tensed very tightly, taking energy away from other muscles as well as hormones that your brain needs to properly function.

CHAPTER 3 – IMPROVING MEMORY

Now that you understand how your memory works on a basic level, you can start to understand how to improve upon that memory. Even if you feel like you don't have any room left to learn, know that your memory is limitless. You have so much potential with how much you know and how much you have left to learn.

BASIC TIPS

There are supplements, therapies, and programs that all might help improve cognitive function, but sometimes, it's just about understanding the basic tips to help actually improve your memory. You can do all of these things or take all the different supplements available that claim to help improve brain function and memory, but if you are not actively trying to improve your thought processes overall, you will never find actual success with improving memory. You have to be actively trying to increase your brain's strength, not just hoping that something will happen one day to trigger your memory.

Distractions are the biggest reasons why someone might have trouble remembering things. If you actually want to improve your memory, you have to make sure that you can first identify distractions. Sometimes, this involves admitting to yourself that something legitimately is distracting you. You might not want to admit that listening to podcasts while studying is distracting you, but you have to in order to make sure that you are giving your attention to what's important.

Other people hope that they can just memorize certain things, but you have to remember that it will take practice to improve your memory. You are not going to become a memorizer overnight, but there actually are memory athletes that know how to memorize a deck of cards in a matter of minutes. It takes practice, and the more effort you put into remembering things, the better off you will be in the end.

There has to be a level of practical application as well. This might involve doing something physical, or just coming up with examples in your brain. You will never be able to easily remember things if you do not associate what you are memorizing with a level of application. We'll look at these ideas further in the next three sections.

Avoid Distractions

Make sure that you are studying or learning in the proper environment. The ideal situation is to have a place completely dedicated to studying and learning, such as an office. Unfortunately, we do not all have access to this, but that doesn't mean you can't learn just as much, if not more, than something that has a massive decked-out office. The brain is still the same whether it is in one place or another, it is just about how easily you can tap into the parts that you need the most.

Clean up around you. If you try to study somewhere messy, you are not doing yourself any favors. Each item that surrounds you at this current moment takes up your attention. The place you are sitting, the clutter in the corner, the dog toys on the floor, the empty water glasses next to your bed; all these things are visual reminders of a task that needs to be done. Though you might be ignoring all the little objects around you that are causing the mess, you are only doing so on your conscious level. Your unconscious is still working hard to pick up on information about those items, deciding how to process the things that they are learning. If you make sure your place is clean and free of any visual reminders of the things that you have to do, you will be better off in the end in terms of learning and remembering.

Turn off the TV and choose music without words. If

you have to sit there and write a boring paper on a subject that doesn't interest you, it can be tempting to just turn on the TV and toss an easily digestible movie or show to fill space and time. Remember that even if you aren't giving it your full attention, it is still taking up some of your focus, meaning you will give less to what you actually have to try and learn.

Music is a great way to help keep you focused, as it drowns out background noise and gives rhythm and repetition to your brain. If you are listening to music while studying, however, make sure that it doesn't have words. Even if you aren't actively listening to the lyrics and what they mean, your unconscious is picking up on the song, meaning less focus will be given to whatever it is you are trying to learn.

Try and delegate a specific space that you study. Even if this means sitting at the opposite end of the couch. You can associate this new spot with your learning center. Every time you have to do homework, work on a project, or even read, do so in this study spot. It can be a different room, the library, or just a random spot in your chair in your house. The most important element to this specified spot is just that it is used only for studying. Do not sit in your bed when you try to learn, or any other spot that is associated with relaxation. Your mind gets used to your patterns of behavior, so if you sit on the left side of the couch to watch movies and binge popcorn, if you sit in this spot to try to study, your mind is going to kick into relaxation mode. However, simply moving to the right side of the couch automatically switches things up in your brain. If you continue to sit in this specified study spot, eventually, your brain will kick into focus mode when you arrive here. Then, even if you are not in a good mood and have no interest in studying, if you plant yourself in this specified spot, your brain might just kick into focus mode automatically.

Practice

Practice is important for every aspect of your life. Many people, especially in today's society, do not have the patience to practice. Instead of trying to practice just one thing, they'll move onto something else. Then they do not want to practice that, so they'll move onto something else. People would rather spend ten hours a week trying new things to distract them or catch their interest instead of just spending one hour a week to improve on a valuable skill.

You might find that you get to a point where you feel like you are not good at anything because the things you try you fail at. With everything, there is a level of failure that should be expected when on the path towards greatness. If you are not willing to practice, you can expect that you also will not see any results.

Practice different games that improve cognitive functions. This could be something simple, like a crossword or sudoku taken from the daily newspaper. You could try more complex games, like a puzzle video game or another system that forces you to think critically harder. You might not be good at the game at first, but the more you practice, the better off you will be in the end.

Practice a healthier lifestyle. If you go and eat a blueberry spinach salad, you are not going to remember your childhood right away. However, if you eat a blueberry spinach salad every day for 30 days, at the end of that month, you will realize that your memory is much better than what it used to be before you started that healthier lifestyle.

Don't expect to memorize something immediately. It will take a few times of repetition to ensure that you remember the information better and properly. If you try to force yourself too hard to remember something, there's a good chance you will get discouraged after you don't succeed, setting yourself up for failure. You might memorize everything you need to know within seconds but remember to not count on this right away. Be realistic with your expectations and practice methods in order to ensure that you do not become continually disappointed in yourself.

There are memory athletes that are capable of this, but it takes PRACTICE to get there!

Make Connections

Connecting new information to things that you already

know can be the greatest way to do something. If you are learning about photosynthesis, for example, then this might involve associating the processes with the houseplant that is sitting in the corner of your room. If you are learning about the first World War, you might associate the notable people involved as being characters on your favorite drama television series. By taking new information and connecting it to the things that we already know, you will be able to make sure that this information is better stored in the long run.

Sometimes, the worst part about studying is that you might have to learn things that you will never use again in your life. Maybe you are studying for the ACT and you have to focus on mathematics, even though you plan to major in history when you head to college. Find a way to make this information that seems pointless, relevant to your life. History that doesn't seem relevant to your current life can be connected to the politics that are currently surrounding us. Math can be exemplified by your shopping habits or weekly budget. Science, well, science is always relevant, but, if you aren't sure of how to remember concepts, connect ideas to things you already know. Humans tend to enjoy talking and thinking about themselves. The best way for you to remember something is to make it relevant to you on a personal level.

Associating certain things with what you already know is best as well. This is more a process of memorization than trying to relate certain concepts to your life. For example, if you are trying to remember all the bones in your body, maybe you will associate each bone with that thing. You might remember that your Humerus is in your upper arm because your friend John is very humorous, and he has a large tattoo on his arm. There is no relevancy of John and his sense of humor to the test you are going to be talking about bones, but you know John and all his jokes, so you will remember that the tattoo on his arm is located on top of his Humerus. Whatever strange way you have to use to remember something, go for it.

There really is no rule for connecting strange ideas. Sometimes, that strange idea is the exact way you need to remember something. For example, maybe you are studying the systems in the body. You can list off the skeletal, nervous, reproductive, muscle, and every other system in your body, but you always forget about the endocrine system. To remember this, maybe think endocrine, like end, like how you want the study session to end. You might not fully grasp the endocrine system and everything it does, but you have at least managed to come up with a unique enough way to remember this system that you will not be forgetting it as an option on the test.

UNDERSTANDING VERSUS KNOWING

In order to improve your memory and accelerate your learning, you have to understand the difference between knowing something and actually understanding it. You know that if you do a certain thing, you will get a certain result, but do you know exactly why?

Think about how many commercials you might have seen, or jingles you have heard repeatedly, without even understanding what the product actually is. You know the product, but do you actually understand what it is and how it works? How many times have you seen a logo for a brand, only to realize years later that it is not the exact picture that you thought?

The more you actually understand something, the better you will be able to know other things, because you have unlocked a practical part of your brain.

This is because of the connections that can be made between various aspects of the learning process. Understanding, at its core, is the process of making connections, applying relevancy, and application if related.

Grasping Concepts

You could memorize all the bones in your body, but if you do not actually understand what those bones do, you might not be able to easily remember them. When you can actually understand why something functions in the way it does, you will be able to easily remember it. You can memorize all the parts of a machine you want, but you will not really get it until you understand how those parts work. Once you do understand something, you are not likely to forget it, which will make studying much easier. Before trying to memorize certain concepts and terms, ask yourself if you even understand it.

The reason why you might take a test and forget the information the next day is because you just memorized something. If you did practice all night for a test, using flashcards and other memorization techniques, you might not always succeed in the test either. You might ace the multiple choice and true or false sections, but if you get to a part that asks for you to give long written answers from applicable questions, you might completely fail. This is because these questions do not require you to recite the order of certain letters that you knew, but instead, you are required to actually apply a method or theory in a practical way, and not everyone will be able to do this.

This starts with actually listening, and not just hearing. Visualizing, not just seeing. Go beyond the surface level. Many people might record lessons, hoping they can just go home later and listen to it again, not having to worry about listening in class. If you are able to actually focus and understand what the professor is saying, you will not even need that recorded lecture. Instead, you can take notes on what they might be breezing over, so you can ask questions at the end of class or do your own personal research on the things that you do not understand.

Contextualize the different concepts that you are learning, do not just try to remember them. Repetition helps, but the easiest way to remember something is to just understand it. You won't' need to memorize definitions from notecards if you can just understand the basic concept behind the process that you are studying.

This might mean developing different parts of your life further as well. Listening and visualizing are important in the classroom, but they can help you learn rapidly in other areas of your life as well. If you focus on listening to different songs, podcasts, or audiobooks, you will end up getting a better understanding afterward than if you just let it be background noise to fill a quiet room.

Using Examples

Use synonyms and examples for how you might plan on understanding a certain concept. Analogies and different wild scenarios will help you better associate various concepts into your life.

Let's take a basic mathematical concept for you to understand how to use examples (notice that we are doing this method right now). Let's say that you have to memorize a certain equation for an upcoming test. The equation might be $2x + y = z$. You tell yourself over and over again that $2x + y = z$. You practice filing in for x, y, and z, and you use repetition to make sure you have the equation down. Then, when it comes time for the test, you are faced with the equation: $(z - y)/2 = x$. This is the same concept, but if you do not actually understand the equation at the core, you will not be able to solve the equation since it is different than the one you memorized. This is a simple example, but it is a way to realize that understanding is so much more important than just memorizing.

Mindfulness

The reason why some of us have so much trouble understanding things is because we are not being mindful. Instead of focusing on what the teacher is saying, we're off daydreaming about the cute person at the front of the class, what we might get for lunch, or even something ridiculous such as the interview we're going to give to Ellen after we get famous.

Mindfulness aims to help someone live in the moment, rather than be trapped in their thoughts about the future and past. We lose hours of our life to fantasizes that aren't real or hold no value. Instead of actually spending time with your friends, you might be trapped in your own insecurities, thinking instead about how much everyone around you might be judging you. The worst form of not being mindful, in terms of learning, is when we're so worried about making sure we take down information about a test that we do not even listen to the professor's lectures.

Instead of actually listening to someone you are having a conversation with, you might instead be trying to picture what you are going to do next. Sometimes, people feel the need to "win," certain conversations, or at least prove that they are smart and have something to say. Most of the time, a friend might just need an ear to vent to, but instead, we offer to give long-winded advice that they'll never take.

The reason why you might have so much trouble remembering certain parts of your life is maybe because you dissociate too often. You will not remember the fun trip you had if you spent the entire time worrying about whether or not you were actually going to have fun!

Being mindful is the greatest way to ensure that you are going to remember what's necessary while cutting out everything that is not. One way to practice mindfulness is to start by picking out a color. Here, I'll pick it out for you: yellow. Now, identify everything that is yellow in the place you currently are. Set the book down and actually do this for a minute or two. There you go! That is being mindful! It is as simple as that. Reading in general is a way to be mindful, but I wanted you to make sure that you got the chance to practice this method.

Another more complex way of being mindful is to tap into all of your senses. This involves:

1. Identify something that you can taste in the room you are in. Maybe it is the glass of soda sitting next to you or a little bit of food left on an almost-empty plate of food. If there's nothing edible around, that doesn't mean you can't still taste something. Maybe it is even something as simple as the top of your hand. You are not supposed to actually taste this item, but instead, just become aware of its presence.

2. Now, pick out two things that you can smell. You do not have to actually be able to identify their scent, but rather, identify two things that you could smell, hypothetically, if you wanted to.

3. Find three things that you can hear. Even if you can't hear them right now, pick out something that makes noise, such as a set of speakers, a phone, or even a spoon and a pot that you can bang together to make a noise.

4. Pick out four things that you can touch. Try to identify different textures, like something wooden, something made of fabric, a cold item, and something bumpy or rough. You do not have to get up and touch these things, but just identify what they would be and what they might feel like.

5. Lastly, look at five different things. These can be the first five things that you see. Identify them and repeat what they are out loud. If you look at the coffee table, say to yourself, coffee table. If you look at your toes, say, my toes.

This all seems simple, but they're all activities that can be really important in grounding us in a moment, taking us away from the thoughts that are consuming all parts of our brain. Next time you are feeling anxious, stressed, or unfocused, practice this method. You will be surprised at how much you are able to pull yourself back into a moment.

Being mindful is a practice. After you do the activity above, you might find that you get anxious again within a matter of minutes. Go ahead and do the mindful activity again and repeat until you have shut those anxious thoughts out of your brain.

TENDING YOUR MEMORY

Think of your memory like a garden. You have to make sure the soil is healthy and ready to be planted. You have to get rid of all the weeds and anything else that is just taking up space. Now, it is time to plant the seeds. You choose seeds that are relevant and are hoping to grow into practical things, such as tomatoes. You might also choose to plant something experimental, like a weird flower. If it doesn't grow, you will not be too disappointed, as you are really focused on the tomato. Then, the plants start to grow, and you have to water them every day to make sure they keep thriving. Once the tomato plant has grown, that doesn't mean you no longer tend to the garden. You might harvest the tomatoes, but you will keep the plant around for continued growth, tending to it day after day, making sure that it only grows larger in the end.

Continual application of these practices and examples is only going to help ensure continued growth for your brain. Confronting past traumas or anything else that might be fogging your brain is like picking away all the weeds. Then, planting the seeds is the acknowledgment of the things that you would like to start to know. After that, watering your garden is like reading books and doing all the studying needed to make sure the idea grows. Then, your "harvest," might be in the form of a big exam or certification process. After that, the knowledge doesn't stop or the requirement for "watering," just as the tomato plant doesn't stop growing.

These practices will help in other areas of your life too, not just in the way that you pass different exams. Make sure that you are tending to all parts of your life as a garden, using patience and care to ensure optimal results. Improving memory should not just be about passing a test. It'll help you live a more fulfilling life overall as well.

Remember Right Away

While being mindful, tell yourself right away that you have to remember something. If you put emphasis on it when you are learning, you are letting your short-term memory know that you have to send something to your long-term memory. Do not get too hung up on this to the point where you start worrying about whether or not you are going to remember something.

Using a physical indicator can help elicit a memory. Maybe when you meet someone new, you tap the inside of your hand subtly, so then when you see that person again, you will remember tapping your hand, which will trigger your memory to recall their name much easier. Do not ever harm yourself when it comes to using memory for a physical reminder. Some people might pinch themselves or dig their nails into their skin to try and remember something. All this does is associate pain with whatever it is you are trying to remember. In order to ensure your brain doesn't have any harmful trauma, it will only work harder to make you forget these things. Use positive touch. This might mean touching something around you as well. Next time you are in a lecture, class, or meeting, and you start to hear something you want to remember, place your hand on whatever sitting method you are using. If you are on a couch or in a big comfy chair, place your hand on the armrest, feeling the threads beneath your finger. If you are in a desk or office chair, place your hand underneath the seat, feeling the plastic or metal underneath your hands. This shouldn't be a grand gesture or anything that takes too much attention from you or others around you. A simple touch is all it takes to really help solidify a memory.

Associate that memory with the environment in which it was learned. When you are taking the test and you get to a part about global warming, you might remember the answer from the day of the lecture when the classroom was especially hot. Being aware of your environment is a form of mindfulness, and it will help you recall information from the time that you learned certain things if you associate them with the place in which they were learned.

Emphasize in your brain the things that you need to hold onto. This is why highlighting can be important when taking notes or reading books. While you should still be sure that you are understanding the concept at the time that you have learned it, highlighting, or writing things down in specific parts of texts will help give you a guideline for when you have to revisit material to study for a test.

You Might Lose it

"Use it or lose it," certainly applies to your brain and how it works. There's a ton in your brain that you will remember without effort. That is why so many people describe certain behaviors as if it is "like riding a bike." This phrase basically refers to the fact that if you learned how to ride a bike as a child, you might not ride one for thirty years, but when you get back onto the two-wheeler, you are a natural, as your brain knows exactly what it needs to do to help make sure you are properly riding the bike.

Certain things might come back to you, but the small details should be tended to or else you are not going to have the same memory you always did. Our brains are so impressionable as children, that the reason why we remember so many things like brushing our teeth, pouring cereal, and riding our bike, is because these things were taught to us as we were discovering how to live in general. These key moments shaped our thought processes and memories, as well as define developmental stages. As we get older, we're much less impressionable, so we will not be as easily able to remember certain things. This is why it is important to tend to our minds, so we do not lose any information that we have worked so hard to gain.

Not the same amount of effort always needs to go into keeping up memories as it took to actually build that memory. You probably have nights you know you will never forget, but make sure that if you do worry about forgetting something, you write it down in a journal. Be expressive with your descriptions too. Sometimes, we might end up remembering a version of what was written down rather than what actually happened, so do your best to describe situations so that you can understand them better later.

Practical application will always help, but make sure you are remembering all the little things that you do not use.

For example, you might be an experienced driver, and maybe you have gone 10 years with a clean driving record. However, if you went to retake the driver's test right now, you might fail, not because you are a bad driver, but because you do not remember the smaller, more practical information that went along. It is not always necessary to know every detail about how to drive, but there are other applicable scenarios that require consistent mental upkeep.

Future Memory Concerns

Diseases like Alzheimer's and Dementia can be terrifying. Being old shouldn't be so scary. You have grown your mind for ages and built a meaningful life, yet so many people fear the elderly because they are afraid of death. The reason that these things are so scary is because of medical issues like dementia and Alzheimer's. To make sure that we're doing our best to avoid anything that makes us fearful of the future, we have to ensure we're doing our best to take care of ourselves now.

These things are not completely curable, but it is important to do your best to avoid any sort of memory loss from happening. Losing your memory is scary, debilitating, and challenging for your loved ones to have to endure as well. Aside from a healthy diet and semi-regular exercise routine, make sure that you are working out your brain as well.

Repetition can be a reason why someone might experience these memory loss conditions. If you do the same thing day after day, never switching up what you do, you are not working out your brain to its full potential. You are stagnant with your cognitive behavior and the knowledge you are taking in has plateaued. Make sure you do something different every single day in order to ensure you are changing things up. This can be as simple as switching the hand that you brush your teeth with or can be something major like going to a different coffee shop to work.

Continually force cognitive development. Do not ever feel satisfied with how much you know, and make sure you are taking everything in at a deep level to ensure that you are not allowing your brain to plateau.

CHAPTER 4 –

CONCENTRATION

Concentration can be the hardest thing for many people to achieve. Even intelligent people that have studied in various educational institutions for years might still find difficulty when it comes to finding the concentration. There are many different factors that go into why or how someone is able to concentrate, so it's important to remember this while going throughout your learning processes.

FOCUSING ATTENTION

Your brain's ability to concentrate on one stimulus is focus. When you can cut out all other distractions and only hone in on one topic, you are better focusing on the things that matter the most.

"Just focus," is something you probably say often to yourself, especially when it comes to studying. It is a concept that is much easier said than done.

Your focus is a reaction to everything around you. It can be hard to give focus to one specific thing. While you are trying to focus on someone talking, your body is also telling you to focus on the fact that your stomach is growling.

Remember that our brains are animalistic. The reason you are distracted by shiny lights or other things around you is because your attention is going towards them to investigate. Does this have value? Does this have meaning? More simply, our animal brains also make us think simple things, like, can I have this, or, can I eat this?

Internal Factors

In order to combat dissociation, make sure you focus on what is important. You have to address internal factors that might be pulling at your attention. Internal factors include anything that goes on in your mind that might take attention away from the things that are important.

How are you feeling emotionally? Are you sad about something that just happened? Going through a breakup, a loss, or any other emotionally disturbing event will be sure to pull at your distraction. You just have to make sure that you have the tools needed to overcome this temporarily, so you can put your focus on something else. Most of the time, focusing on specific things help to make sure that you are distracted from the thing that was upsetting you in the first place.

Do you have the motivation it takes to learn this certain topic? If you have no interest in the concept or idea that you are studying, you are not going to be able to properly focus. Find ways to make even the most uninteresting topics interesting and relevant to your life.

Are your basic human needs currently met? If you are cold or hungry, your brain is going to think about that. Make sure you are well-rested, fed, and at the right temperature to ensure that no other basic need is going to keep you distracted from learning.

External Factors

The external factors of an environment are important as well. You can't always control these things, but you should try to turn your attention away from them.

Is there construction happening right outside your window? The drilling, clanging, banging, and yelling that comes along with construction can be enough to make you want to give up on it all. Invest in some headphones, or schedule study times for when you know the workers will not be around.

An external distracting factor could even be the color of the room. If you are in a shockingly red room, you might not have as much focus as when you are in a place with more relaxed colors on the wall.

Who's teaching you counts as an external factor. If you can't stand your professor, you are not going to learn the proper information in an easy way. Do your investigations needed to make sure that you are properly finding people that are suited for you? Ask others that have taken classes if they enjoyed the professor before you sign up for the class. If your only option is to take a class with someone you do not like, look for study groups, or sessions taught by teaching assistants, in order to make sure you are still taking in the information you need.

Focusing on Focus

When you tell yourself, "just focus," you are not going to be able to always do that. When you are hungry, you can't just tell yourself to stop being hungry. You have to fix the problem at the core to make sure you are getting the best resolution.

Make yourself aware of the distractions. Ask why they are so important in blocking you from learning other information. Is checking up on your social media more important than studying for the test?

Be mindful and focus on the moment, not what's going to happen next or what has happened before.

Give yourself time to be distracted. Instead of trying to just go five hours for studying, give yourself five, ten, or fifteen-minute breaks in between long sections to make sure that you are not going to end up running completely off track because you got lost for too long on Instagram. Always give yourself the chance to be distracted, but make sure you are doing so in a planned amount of time.

TAPPING INTO YOUR BRAIN

Your brain is a tool. It is also like a muscle that needs to be exercised. The more you work it out, the stronger it will be. It is continuously working, and it is not like it is going to get "fat." You still have to make sure that you are exercising it to keep it at an optimized performance.

All of the information we learn about our brains comes from someone else's brain. It is not like we are excavating caves in the hope of finding some written manual on our brain. If we do, then it is something that was written by a brain! There is no magic key for how to use your brain, but there are important steps in making sure you are keeping up with all that is important in growing cognitive function.

You hold so much potential inside the squishy stuff between your skull. It is crazy to think of what that mind is capable, and everything we still have yet to learn.

Explore your own brain like you would the world. Next time you are eating something, ask why you like it. It is easy to go to the fridge and grab some ice-cream. But as you scoop yourself a bowl, ask why you like it. Is it if the flavor? The texture? The cold? Always question your behavior, even if it is something simple that you have always been doing. You might think you have retrieved all the information necessary from a specific scenario, but you have to understand how much more you have to learn.

Exercising the Muscle

You can focus all you want on building your pecs and glutes at the gym, but if you do not give any attention to your brain, what's the point? No matter how little junk food you eat, how much time you put in at the gym, and what supplements, creams, and lotions you use to enhance your appearance, what's the point if your brain is weak? If you do not know that much in general, or if you are continually stressed out and anxious, everything else is so much harder. Always strive to work out your brain as you would any other part of your body.

Be wary of "training" software. Lumosity was advertised as being a great tool to help you build your brain, but they ended up having to shell out a multi-million-dollar settlement because the practices weren't that legit. They promised that certain mental ailments, such as the general effects of aging as well as dementia and Alzheimer's, would be reduced if you played their games throughout certain periods in a week. They had no science to back this up, and instead just fed off the fears of their users in order to make a quick buck.

The best way to make sure your brain is improving is to change things up. Even switching the route that you drive to work can help make sure you are not getting too stuck in certain rituals and patterns that might end up leading to decreased brain function later on.

The more senses you involve in any brain strengthening activity, the better. Something that requires physical touch, listening, and seeing, are great activities to help make sure you are giving your brain the workout it needs and deserves.

Learn a hobby. Learning how to play an instrument is a great way to make sure plenty of senses are being touched on, but overall, you should try to at least incorporate one hobby into your life. This could be something simple like doing a puzzle once a week, or even just going for a daily walk.

Test your brain with memorization tricks and mathematical scenarios. Count how many light bulbs there are on a string of lights or memorize your grocery list. When you give yourself little tests throughout the day, you will be able to much more easily improve your memory and cognitive function overall.

Becoming Aware

The more self-aware you are, the better off you are in every aspect of your life, not just the way you learn.

Being aware is the practice of using mindfulness while making yourself fully conscious of a concept. Not many people understand how to be self-aware, which can sometimes be rather startling.

Being aware helps you become a better person. You start to recognize how your actions affect others, and you look for ways in which you can be more helpful overall to those around you.

You can combat different brainwashing techniques, or ways others have been manipulating you. If you are aware of all the methods advertisers have been using to sell us products, you will be less likely to fall for them.

You can become more open-minded as you continually learn new things. You will start to realize how small yet how impactful each individual is, growing from these thoughts into broader and more logical ideas.

You will also be able to learn more things in general, putting more attention towards the things that matter most. The more aware you are, the more mindful you are, which will make it much easier to not only learn new things, but to remember them as well.

Suffering and Clinging

Oh, how we all suffer. It presents itself in different ways, but we all experience a level of suffering. You might have suffered today when you were forced awake by your alarm clock. Maybe you suffered to deal with your mental illness, struggling to feed and bathe yourself. You might even be suffering deeply right now from a loss of a close relative. No matter what you might be experiencing, you at least understand on some level what it means to suffer.

The reason why we suffer can be associated with our level of clinging. This is based on Buddhist teachings from philosopher Phra Dharmakosacarya, who is also known as Buddhadasa Bhikkhu. The intention of discovering why we might grasp and cling, is so we can reach a higher level of understanding, separating ourselves from the things that cause us to suffer.

Various levels of clinging can be separated into four different categories. The first is sensual, which involves any object that is desirable to us. We cling to things that we like and that bring us joy.

The second is our attachment to different opinions. We cling to the thoughts our parents instilled in us, as well as the views from our society that shape the way we think.

The third is the attachment to ritual. This involves any

ritual we cling to, such as weddings and holidays.

The fourth is attachment to ourselves. We cling to our own perspective, making sure that anything that has meaning does so to us first more than anyone else.

If you identify why you might be suffering, you can more easily combat that. Are you suffering because you do not have an object you want? Do you suffer come because you are having combative thoughts with the different opinions we were taught? Maybe we have begun suffering because we are stressed over a certain tradition. Most often, we suffer because we cling to the idea that the world owes us something.

Suffering is seen through stress and anxiety, sadness and remorse. When we can work through this level of suffering, we can make sure our minds are clear and ready to learn and memorize.

Eliminating yourself from suffering, whether it is induced by stress, worry, or anxiety, will only help in the end when it comes to personal development.

REDUCING STUDY TIMES

The most challenging part with education is all the time that has to go into studying and learning. Whether you are in college, graduated, or never went, you know on at least some level that it is about having fun and meeting new people. The reality is, however, that many students have to spend hours a day in their room or at the library studying.

It is not always the level of material that makes it difficult to study. Sometimes, how much time you put in is just based around whether or not you are studying in the proper way. The most effective students are sometimes the ones that study the least. This is because they make sure to understand the information when it was first taught to them instead of focusing on how and when they're going to study.

What works for many people does not for others, and that is crucial to remember. You have to be ready to accept a trial and error phase when it comes to testing out different study methods and the ways in which you learn different information.

Remember to confront your inner self before you study and try to make sure you are in a good place with both internal and external factors resolved. Eliminate distractions, reduce stress, and feed yourself to make sure that you can put all your attention towards studying.

The easiest way to reduce study time is to actually pay attention in class in the first place. Next time you head to a class or an important meeting, no matter how much you might be dreading sitting there and listening, be prepared to do so to ensure that you do not have to put in the work later.

Repetition

Repeating things is the best way to make sure that you are improving memory. This can be done with flashcards or by reading certain texts over again. The more you repeat something and allow it to pop into your life numerous times, the better you will remember in the end.

When you meet someone, you will find that remembering their name is much easier if you repeat it back to them. If they say, "Hello, I'm Jenny," you should reply with, "Hello Jenny, I'm ___, nice to meet you." By saying Jenny out loud, you have given yourself the repetition needed to hopefully remember her name.

Writing things down is a good way to elicit a higher level of remembering something. Take certain notes from class and rewrite them later on in order to give some repetition. You should try to switch up the words but stick to the same ideas overall to make sure that you are repeating the necessary information.

Variation

Variation is the greatest way to improve memory. This is because you are constantly increasing cognitive function. Instead of reminding yourself of things that you already know, you are forcing your brain to think in a new and innovative way to confront a certain issue or digest some new information.

If you are trying to build muscle mass, you are not going to do so by lifting the same amount of weights day after day. Muscle confusion is a great way to ensure you're building mass and switching up from leg to arm day is a way the top athletes ensure they do not plateau in their workouts.

Use different sources. While studying for specific tests is important, you should also make sure that you are using outside sources. Though you might be taking a test on a specific text and you have a teacher that drafts things close to the same phrasing in the reading, using a different source still might help to ensure that you are actually understanding the concepts better, so you can apply them should you forget a certain word or phrase.

YouTube and Google offer great ways and methods for learning. You can find free articles and videos on literally any subject in order to ensure you are getting a certain amount of variation into your study routine.

Allow Rest

Let's say that today is Monday, and in one week, you have an exam. Maybe you have to work tonight, Wednesday, Friday, and Saturday. Then you have four other assignments you are working on Tuesday and Thursday. For this reason, it would be tempting to get all your studying in on Sunday.

Do not do this! It is better to make sure that instead of forcing yourself to study for 10 hours straight, you give yourself the chance to study for at least an hour a day until the test. Then, Sunday can just be your review day where you make sure any area of weakness is emphasized.

Do not put studying off because you are afraid you are going to forget everything. You will not forget the information if you learn it in a way that compliments understanding rather than focusing on memorization. Although it is hard to study once a day for a week, it'll be so much better in the long run than staying up all night Sunday to learn everything at once. You need rest in between study sessions so that your brain can better process and solidify the information that it is consuming.

Remember that lack of sleep can cause poor memory. Sometimes, you might be tempted to stay up all night, but if the test is in the morning, you are not doing yourself any favors.

CHAPTER 5 – QUICK LEARNING TIPS

With so much information available to us, it's important to know how to take information in quickly so that we can continually expand on what we know. Some people learn slow, others can learn with a snap of the finger. No matter what your pace, everyone can benefit from tips to learn much faster.

SWITCH IT UP

We have already stressed plenty how important variation is, but now let's get into some different tips for how you can better implement variation into your routine. The more you can differentiate the various things that you do to a day to day basis, the more that you will be able to improve overall cognitive function. When this is done, learning and memorization will soon follow, leading to a more well-rounded mind.

This can start by physically switching up your environment. If you have been sitting at your desk all day and you have no idea how you are going to finish a project, start by switching up where you are working. Take your laptop to a coffee shop or maybe even the library. Going to places like these not only help give you a fresh environment to help encourage more work, but you will also be surrounded by other people that are also working which will help make you more motivated to get stuff done. If you can't leave and do not have the option to do work elsewhere, then try just changing the position in which you are sitting. Turn your computer around and sit on the other side of your desk or try even kneeling instead of sitting at your chair. Of course, you do not want to do this too long to the point where you hurt yourself but changing things up will wake up your brain and kick you back into a place where you can better focus on what needs to be done rather than all the distractions surrounding you.

Recognize when you have hit a plateau. Track your progress to make sure that you are continually learning, and if you are not noticing any improvement, there's a good chance that you have hit a stopping point in the way that you are learning. Remember that a plateau doesn't mean that you are no longer capable of learning something. It just means that you need to change up how you are getting that information. This is either the effect of making your brain fall into too repetitive of a pattern, or it can just be disinterest and lack of motivation in a subject.

If a method is not working, do not force it. If you have spent 2 hours making notecards, but actually studying them doesn't help, then you might just have to admit that this is not the method that is going to work.

Understand that it is time that is not wasted. You still wrote things down which is helpful. You just have to be aware when something is not working so you can find something that is.

Use Different Sources

Optimize where you are getting your information. The sources that you choose to use will be very important in determining if you will actually gain any knowledge from a subject or if you will just keep getting the same things you have already been receiving.

If you read an article, click on the hyperlinks to understand something better. The writer might have a way of twisting the words around to make things more sensational. Never base a bit of knowledge on a headline either. Something that reads, "Study Shows Your Dog Hates You," might just be taken from a small study in which one researcher found their dog gave them a dirty look. Many articles are dependent on getting clicks to drive advertisement prices, so they'll take the teensiest bit of information and turn it into a national panic, just so they can get more hits.

Even if you are studying for a specified test, let's say, for a book like *Great Expectations*, you should still switch up your sources. This might include watching the movie or finding a Reddit thread that discusses this book. If you didn't understand a concept, or even just missed a certain instance of foreshadowing, you might find useful information online that will only improve your overall comprehension. Anyone in a learning environment needs to realize just how lucky they are to have access to all of the useful sources that exist on the internet.

The more sources you use, the better you will be in the end. Do not forget to utilize free things, such as online courses or instructional videos. If you do not have a hobby, make learning your activity of choice!

Change Your Perspective

Make sure you look at something in a different way than you did before in order to get a better understanding. The more perspectives you have on a subject, the better you will be able to view it for what it actually is. What you might see as a great idea, someone else might see as a disaster, and vice versa. Maybe the best course of action is a middle place between solution and disaster.

Maybe you're the boss of a company, and you just do not know how to improve sales. Perhaps you could choose to look at your worst salesperson, asking them what they need to improve. A good leader, or just learner in general, is someone who knows the value of other people's opinions. Not everyone will have the great ideas you need, but they'll still at least offer a view that you might have never considered before.

Use opposing perspectives for information as well. For example, if you are writing a persuasive speech, use the opposite perspective as your framework. For example, if you are writing a paper on how great bananas are, you might look at sources that discuss how awful and dangerous bananas can be. You can find a framework within these different teachings while also making sure that you build a stronger argument for your perspective.

Do not Focus on One Topic

While it is tempting to just stick to one idea when you are studying, make sure you are implementing many. Focus on the things that you do not understand, but do not overlook basic information you assume you know. You might end up missing something important in the process.

For example, if you are studying the body, and you do not particularly understand the endocrine system, do not force yourself to study this further. Instead, look to the other systems as a way to increase variation and perspectives. If you learn how the reproductive or digestive system works, it might tie into the parts of the endocrine system that you do not understand.

Always revisit topics that confuse you, but make sure that you are still focusing on multiple subjects. This will keep your mind active and prevent any plateauing that could occur if you stick to just one thing to learn.

If you limit your mind, you are limiting how much you are going to learn. You are setting boundaries and limitations on the things that you let into your life while restricting the things you already know as well. Do not let yourself fall into a fixed mindset. Make sure you are following a path towards continued development and positive change.

This includes topics that might not interest you as well. You might discover you actually like a certain idea or thing that you otherwise avoided because it wasn't initially appealing. Expose yourself to things that you aren't particularly fond of in order to make sure you are not limiting yourself too much. At the very least, you will still learn one important thing after consuming media you dislike.

PRACTICAL TECHNIQUES

Looking inward is important, but sometimes, you just need some practical techniques to help you learn better. If you have a test next week, you might not have the time it takes to actually practice all the things necessary to elicit a huge change in the way you study, so you will just want to incorporate some practical tips to ensure you are doing the best you can to ace the test.

Practical techniques are going to be the most important in making sure that you are actively trying to learn more. This includes anything that forces you to take the information you know and apply it in a way that is relevant and important.

It starts by making sure you have the right supplies. This includes a notebook, a calculator, pens and pencils, highlighters, note cards, snacks, and anything else needed to help optimize your study sessions. If you go in empty-handed, you will feel unprepared, which will lead to distraction. In order to make sure you are staying focused on your knowledge goals, do not be afraid to overprepare. It is much better than being flustered because you can't stop thinking about all the things you are missing.

Do not wait until the last minute to practice any of these things. Procrastination is just a way that you are torturing your future self! Do things now, starting right after you have finished the book. Do not be afraid to learn! That should be your goal, after all. There is no negative aspect of studying. Even if you never use certain information practically in your day to day life, you have still taken in that information and it can lead to a better understanding of other topics as well.

Start small if you have to. If you can only handle studying twenty minutes a day, that is perfectly fine, so long as you are not planning to cram last minute. The more you study, the easier it will get. Make studying enjoyable so that it is not so hard to do next time. If you find a method that doesn't feel like torture, you will find that it is not so bad in the end.

Write it Down

Humans are the only animals that write things down. Many animals leave their marks and other signs that they were there, but it is not always intentional. We have been writing things down for centuries, and no matter how many keyboards surround us, we're never going to stop.

Writing things down is a practice that involves many important sensory indicators. You have to feel the pencil in your hand as well as the paper underneath the markings that you are doing. You have to use your eyes to focus on what's being written down. Sometimes, you might even smell the paper or hear the way the pen scratches the surface. By using all of these senses, you are taking control of your mind, making sure that it better remembers certain bits of information.

It improves memory to write things down as well. It is a form of repetition to take the things you know and write them down again. It also helps to write phrases professors are saying in various classes, so you can make sure that you are allowing repetition in at the immediate instance that you are learning something.

It improves focus. Instead of letting your mind wander to the darkest corners of your brain, you have given it a task. Now, instead of memorizing and focusing on the content, you have to actually make sure that you are paying attention to how and what you are writing, allowing for all other distractions to fade away.

Read Out Loud

Just like writing is beneficial, so is reciting things out loud. Try and remember the lyrics to a song that you do not sing, versus one that you hum out in the car.

You can better focus when you read things aloud, as all the focus is going into making sure that certain things are traveling from your mind to your voice.

You might understand better as you have been forced for proper pronunciation. When you just skip over words you do not know how to pronounce, you might not incorporate them into your study methods. The best way to avoid this is to learn how to pronounce a word, then say it outlined over and over again in order to finally understand its actual meaning.

You can have fun with studying in this way as well. Say things out loud in a funny voice, or maybe you make up a ridiculous song to go along.

Get your blood pumping by speaking out loud too. Speaking loudly can scare some people, which will start a rush of adrenaline. If you force yourself to stand while talking, that will be even better in terms of how much you are allowed to say and get away with.

Doing this is a great way to practice social skills, meaning you are multitasking without taking the focus away. Sometimes, we simply fear public speaking because we do not speak enough! Improve your speech and overall languages so that everyone can better understand what you might be trying to say at any given moment.

Foods That Help Learning

Eating is one of the best parts of life, and it is also important in helping to make sure that you are learning properly as well! Our brain needs food just like every other part of our body. While it loves glucose, you have to make sure you are only giving your brain food low in fat and in refined sugar. Instead, opt for more whole foods that contain only one or two ingredients.

Your brain is about 3/5ths fat. By eating healthy fatty foods, like fish, you are providing your brain with more omega-3 fatty acids. If you do not like eating fish, you might want to consider taking fish oil pills.

Coffee is a great food for learning. You just have to be careful with how you are consuming it. Coffee will help increase alertness, sharpen concentration, and improve your overall mood. Choose black coffee or coffee without sugary creamer at least, as this will just set you back without providing anything all that substantial.

Berries, like blueberries or blackberries, are full of anti-inflammatory properties that will help reduce inflammation in the brain that might be causing a lack of understanding.

Any food high in antioxidants will give these benefits as well. Antioxidants are crucial and combating the inflammation that can lead to other serious health risks.

While your personal taste is different than others, look for foods that have these important nutrients:

Copper – This is beneficial in aiding in your brain's nerve signals. Animal organs, oysters, nuts, and seeds all contain high levels of copper. You could also just take this supplement, like the others on the list as well.

Iron – Those who are iron deficient will likely have a higher level of brain fog. Low iron will also make you tired, making it very difficult to study at all. Leafy greens like spinach, lentils and beans, and even dark chocolate contain high levels of iron needed to make sure you aren't iron deficient.

Magnesium – This is an important nutrient for improving memory. Whole grains, nuts, seeds, and bananas all have high levels of magnesium.

Zinc – Zinc helps improve nerve signaling overall. To

get some extra zinc in your diet, consider taking vitamin pills or eating foods like the following: chickpeas, beef, and yogurt.

SPEEDY LEARNING

Speedy learning is an important part of continual growth. We do not always have the time to sit down and dedicate hours to learning something new, but that doesn't mean we shouldn't try learning at all. If you go too fast with certain information, you might not remember anything important anyway. There are still ways, however, that you can make sure that you are constantly learning new and important information.

Remember that there are going to be difficult times in studying, and you are going to have to cut through all of it. The key to speeding through is to just focus all of your attention at the thing you are trying to learn. You might realize you run into spots when you are studying where you get distracted. Maybe you decide to check out your phones, or you get caught up looking at your nails and picking cuticles. Perhaps you end up taking five hours for a task that should only take one, all because you couldn't maintain focus. If you stay directed towards one specific goal, you'll be able to much better learn something at a quicker rate.

Create plans for what and how you are going to learn. If you lay out a timeframe in which you want to learn something, you can be certain that you'll be able to tackle it better in the long run. Do not be so strict, however, that you end up panicking because you can't fulfill that goal in the end. Go easy on yourself and set light goals, but still keep in mind the importance of having a solid framework for success.

Remember to be independently specific with your learning processes. Take tips from other people and practice different methods of studying but alter them so that they're specific to you. Focus on your wants, needs, and everything else that has to go into making sure that you are studying.

Focus on what you do not know the most. You have to make sure that you are putting attention towards the things you do not understand so that you can have a consistent level of knowledge in all areas.

Set realistic expectations. Do not be too hard on yourself if you do not follow through with your certain goals. You want to make sure that you do not beat yourself up for simply not knowing something. The easiest way to make sure you are keeping the right attitude is to reward yourself. Congratulate when you reach certain study or work milestones, making sure that you understand how proud you should be for learning new and valuable information.

Simplify

In order to better understand something, pretend as though you would explain it to a five-year-old. This way, you can strip it down to its core to better understand the basic function and purpose instead of getting hung up on all the mechanics involved in the learning processes.

If you do not know how to do this, you can look up online, Explain Like I'm Five, a popular teaching tool that was started on Reddit. This shouldn't be your basis for how you learn everything, but it can certainly help make sure you do not get too caught up on some of the confusing parts of certain subject matter.

Break concepts down into a smaller bit of information.

If you do not understand the entire idea, try taking it step by step until you can ensure you get the whole picture. It can seem tedious to start small, as well as time-consuming. However, it will take less time to properly learn something in small steps rather than sit and struggle for hours while you try to grasp a basic concept.

Separate what you do and do not understand. Write down a list of the things you understand the most, and a list of the things that are most confusing. This will help you determine if you need to ask your teacher for help, or if there are any online sources you can use to help teach you more about a certain subject.

Question the purpose of the information you are learning. When you look at an issue such as a problem-solution, you will be able to understand the big picture in the end.

Summarize

When reading over text, the best way to study it after is to summarize. Write down the summary of everything you read so you can go back and reference different texts while you are studying.

Leave bits of information out that you do not feel are important. Add page numbers to the important bits so that you can reference things easily when needed. The more you write, the more you will remember, but do not add extra things that are only going to take up more time.

Combine thoughts that go together, and even compliment understanding. Summarizing is a way to condense.

Look at the beginning and last sentence of a particular paragraph. Decide, are these the most important bits of information, or is the writer just using transition sentences? If you understand the writer's style for a certain text, you can better break down the information and consume it on the original level it was intended to teach.

Highlight sentences, but also, highlight specific words. Use these keywords to google more specific and relevant information.

CHAPTER 6 – CHANGING MINDSET

The most important part of learning new things is making sure you're in the mindset to do so. You won't hold any value on learning if you're not in the right headspace to do so. This last chapter will take you through the steps necessary to change your mindset towards one that welcomes growth and denies negative consistency.

The Dangers of a Fixed Mindset

A fixed mindset is one that is seeking validation for the thoughts and opinions that they already have. Instead of searching for inner growth and improvement, a person with a fixed mindset will instead try to look for sources to validate the things that they already know.

This creates a mind that is susceptible to disappointment and other negative feelings. If you have a fixed mindset, that means you are likely not allowing new ideas and expectations into your life. You have preconceived ideas of how something should happen, so you are dependent on the comfortability, even feeling out of whack if something doesn't go your way.

Self-awareness is not something that is always present in a fixed mindset. Those that are stuck in their ways aren't going to be as aware of the things around them, or what's inside themselves that causes certain thoughts and emotions. The danger here is that there will be no continual growth without improving your mindset.

Opportunity will not be as present for those with a fixed mindset. They'll instead focus clearly on the things that they already know, clinging to normal and never allowing advancement into their lives.

A fixed mindset is one that is accepted a level of average, mediocrity, and unhealthy consistency. There's nothing wrong with enjoying a certain level of normalcy. Not everyone has to go rock climbing or skydiving every other day. If you are someone that is consistently basic, however, just waking up, going to work, coming home, watching the same thing on TV, and going to bed only to do it over and over and over again for decades at a time, you aren't living to your fullest potential. This reason alone can stunt growth and make it hard to remember certain bits of information.

A fixed mindset is most commonly associated with a bigot. People will usually look at someone racist or homophobic and think they have a fixed mindset. This is true, but even those that describe themselves as open-minded might still be fixed in their ways if they don't allow new ideas and perspectives into their lives.

A Growth Mindset

A growth mindset is one that you should constantly aim for. This is the best way to make sure that you are improving relationships, amounts of knowledge, and just an overall a higher satisfaction in your life.

A growth mindset is more enjoyable, seeking positivity from even the worst parts of life. Even if something doesn't go your way or you have to go through a challenging experience, someone with a growth mindset is still able to see the benefit of the worst situations. If you lose your wallet, it is a very terrifying thing that can disrupt a ton of other factors in your life. With a growth mindset, you'll understand that once lost, it is not a situation that can be changed, and you'll instead look at this experience as a lesson learned. You'll never again let your wallet out of your sight.

At the core, a person with a growth mindset is comfortable with change and has accepted their own imperfections. Change is only scary because we can't easily make predictions about what might happen. Change should be welcomed, as sometimes, it is the only way for things to grow. Think of your mind as a garden again. Perhaps this time, it is about planting seeds inside. You'll probably start off with a small container, and as the plant grows, you move it to a new container. You'll keep switching the home of the plant so that it can continue to grow. If you would have stopped at a small container, the plant wouldn't have outgrown it, it would have just stopped growing. This is the way our mind works. If we do not move onto bigger and better ideas, we'll stay in a fixed mindset forever, so change is the only way these things are going to be allowed into your life.

Relationships improve with a growth mindset. Instead of holding grudges or starting small fights, you can more easily look at the bigger picture to determine what the real issue might be. Once you have tackled a problem at its core, you'll be better equipped to overcome the issue, improving your relationships in the end.

Most importantly, in terms of what this book has been discussing, memory and your ability to learn improves greatly with a growth mindset. When you allow yourself to become free of restrictions, you'll likely be less distracted overall, moving onto a place where you can take information in and understand it right away, storing it in your long-term memory.

THINKING CREATIVELY

Those with a growth mindset will usually think creatively often. This doesn't mean coming up with plot ideas or constantly painting new things. While those activities are creative, creative thinking aims more towards forcing you to "look outside the box." Do not look at things only in the way in which they were taught to you. Instead, aim to find a better perspective overall in which you can get new ideas for innovation and conflict resolution.

Thinking creatively allows you to broaden your perspective, allowing better problem-solving and the ability to overcome obstacles. Instead of looking at something for what it is, look at how it is made up. What's the cause and effect, the root issue, the core truth? From there, you can alter it into something completely new.

Creative thinking allows variation, and by this point, we all know how important that is. The more you switch something up, the more organic, fresher, and newer it will be in the end.

You will be less stressed out when you think creatively. You allow your mind to become free, not as worried about time or outcome. You understand the most important aspect in your thinking process is not the outcome, but the journey in which you get there. That A on the exam is going to feel great, but if you are studying to be a nurse, there's much more at stake than just the letter on your report card.

The next sections will go over some ways that you can start to think creatively.

Brainstorming

Brainstorming starts with a question. What is the essay you are writing about? What is the purpose of this creative project? Put yourself in someone else's perspective and imagine what question they might have about the thing that you are creating, or the solution you are trying to provide.

Brainstorming involves trial and error, and you have to accept that you are going to have some bad ideas in the

Think of an invention that really surprises you, vie or show you love watching. Do you think the r thought of that within a matter of minutes? Stephen King has stated he wrote *The Shining* in one night, but he probably just means he wrote the first draft in one night. And even if he did write that best-selling book in a small timeframe, he had written other books before that helped to improve his skills.

Once you have brainstormed, remember that you do not have to expand upon every idea. In the same breath, do not throw away an idea just because you do not think it is important. Creative thinkers know how to properly edit while also looking at how an idea they already had can be twisted into something new and more valuable.

In the end, don't be too hard on yourself. Creative thinkers treat themselves with the same respect they would give other friends, classmates, or colleagues, because they know that positive reinforcement is much more effective than bullying, belittling, and berating.

Investigate Every Idea

Our brains are endless streams of thoughts and it pretty much never stops. Even in our sleep, we are thinking of new ideas. Some of your favorite books or movies might have even been someone's nightmare at one point. Remember that not every single thought we have is something substantial enough to need attention.

You do not have to give validation to every thought you have. Instead, investigate that thought. For example, on a day-to-day basis, you might have a negative thought about yourself. Maybe you hate your hair, face, clothes, or another part of your body. When you think to yourself, "I'm so ugly," etc. do not validate that thought. Instead, investigate why you had that thought. Who said you were ugly? Was it a bully? A sibling? Maybe even a parent? More often than not, you'll realize most ideas started in your own head. The better you can think on an investigative level, the easier it will be to combat certain ideas that you do not like.

The more you practice this method of investigation, the likelier you will be to combat negative thoughts and expand on the positive ones. This is crucial in cutting down distractions and increasing focus.

Connecting Ideas

Human beings love labeling things and making connections. We are the only animals that are capable of doing this. We can twist information to be relevant towards us, and we can link ideas we might never have thought could be connected.

When you can start connecting ideas, you will improve your knowledge and learning skills all around. The more you can make connections to certain thoughts and ideas, the more you'll realize that you can start to understand things better at their fundamental level.

Do not look at everything on an individual level. Look for how certain things might be related. Every experience, person, and moment is unique. That doesn't mean it can't still be connected to something else relevant at the same time.

This will help you understand things better, which leads to a higher amount of memorization as well. When you can actually understand things at their core and relate them to relevant information, you will not have to worry about writing things down on flashcards. Instead, it'll come naturally to you.

THINKING ANALYTICALLY

Creative thinking is crucial, but sometimes, you also have to make sure you are keeping an analytic viewpoint. If you only allow yourself to think creatively and freely, you might miss some important information that can be very effective on different parts of your life.

Thinking analytically is used in order to solve a problem, or to improve knowledge. A problem doesn't have to be confronted with either analytic or creative thinking. If you can incorporate both methods, you'll find the best practices for learning new information.

This involves organizing thoughts, looking at how ideas might be connected scientifically and categorizing things for optimization. An analytic thinker might use facts, numbers, and statistics to come up with ideas and assumptions based around certain things.

Analytic thinking will also involve a lot of troubleshooting. What parts are bad and what parts are good? It's as simple as that. An analytic thinker might come up with a prediction for a certain scenario, knowing that they're going to have to incorporate a trial and error phase to make sure that they get the best outcomes in the end.

Analytic thinking involves more scientific aspects, with facts based on science and mathematics. While looking at something creatively is important, you also have to know when it is time to face the truth based on legitimate scientific studies.

Breaking Down Problems

If you have to come up with a solution to a problem, you might first choose to look at it analytically. Why did I get a 60 percent on this test? Well, probably because I only devoted 1 hour to study this and instead devoted

12 hours to playing video games.

When it comes to breaking down a problem, there are a few common steps the best analyzers will incorporate.

First and foremost, identify the issue. This sounds obvious, but sometimes, you have to actually state what the main problem is before you start coming up with a solution. Let's use the example of getting a D on a test. The problem might seem like a low score. The real issue, however, is the lack of time that went into studying.

The next step will be to list all of the possible reasons that problem might have occurred. Maybe a new video came out. Perhaps there was a lack of motivation to start studying because of disinterest in the subject. By this point, many people might even be able to dissolve the issue.

If not, the next step would be to identify any and all solutions. List out things that have worked in the past for others, things that have worked in the past for you, predictions about what the best resolve might be, and a way in which you can realistically incorporate what you determine the best solution to be.

Remember that there might be a trial-and-error phase. When approaching issues and logical thinking, you are still going to be wrong a few times like you were when you were creatively thinking. Always remind yourself that there's nothing wrong with small failures or slipping up every now and then.

Looking at Cause and Effect

Analytic thinkers know how to identify cause and effect. This is important for continual learning, problem preparation, and solution building.

Cause is anything that happens "since" or "because." Effect is "therefore" or "so." Since it rained last night, there is ice on the ground. The ice is slippery, so I fell when walking to work.

Sometimes, you might have to start with the effect before you find the cause. If you identify what happened to be the effect of something, you'll be able to easily point out the cause.

It is equally important to list all of the effects that might happen from a certain cause. Identify a cause before it has the chance to affect anything and identify all of the possible outcomes.

Analyzing Outcomes

Analytic thinkers know how to analyze certain outcomes. This occurs from both breaking down problems as well as looking at certain causes and effects.

Be aware of how your present self affects your future self. Right now, you want to just sit and watch TV, but really, you know you have to get studying. Take care of your future self by studying now so that you can watch TV later as a reward. Treat yourself like you would your best friend. Would you make the person closest to you wait to get work done they asked you to do?

In order to grow your mind, make sure that you are analyzing the outcome of every situation. Before making any decisions, figure out how your decision will change the things around you.

This should not be a method that scares you. Sure, when planning an international vacation, a possible outcome might be the plane crashing, you get kidnapped and trafficked, or you catch an incurable blood disease. These are all possibilities but remember to analyze the likelihood as well. None of these things are likely to happen, though you can be prepared for them by making sure you travel safely, become aware of the area you are visiting, and take the proper preventative measures so as not to catch anything on the trip.

TOOLS FOR CONTINUOUS LEARNING

Never stop learning. Remember that when you think you have learned enough from a subject, it is probably just that you have hit a plateau with how you are learning. Always look for ways in which you can continually grow.

Make sure to utilize every tool that is made available for your continuous growth. We have an unlimited amount of information at the tip of our fingers, and yet many people choose to instead just stare at pictures of other people all day. You have to give your mind a break, and there's nothing wrong with social media. You have to make sure, however, that you are not devoting all your time to distractions and never focusing on actually learning anything new and valuable.

A growth mindset will be one that involves a nonstop stream of new information. If you limit yourself, stick to one source, and do not self-reflect, you will get stuck in a fixed mindset.

Those that are good learners with a high memory know

that continuous learning is very important. The more you know, the easier it will be to learn new information, and the more likely you'll be to remember that information in the end as well.

Set No Limits

Sometimes you might get burnout on a subject or your brain just feels tired. Do not let this be a sign that you have a limit. You just have a limit for that day with how much you might be able to take in.

Do not shut any topic out of your life. No matter how uninteresting something might sound, give it a chance. You could discover your new hobby in the process.

Once you achieve a goal, set a new one. It can be tempting to just be satisfied when you achieve a small dream, but just know that this is a signal that it is time to set a newer, even bigger goal.

Life is all about creating new limits and destroying the ones that already exist.

Learning from Outside Sources

Make sure you do not stick to just the internet to get your information. The internet is no doubt the greatest tool there is in our current time for receiving information. However, just like everything else in our lives, we can fall into a place of comfortability.

Maybe you only go to Vice, CNN, or Fox online for your news. While the value in these sites is subjective, the truth is, they only offer one perspective based on their format and style.

Make sure to expose yourself to things you might think you do not like. You will either learn that you do like that thing, or you will only validate what you don't like even more.

Remember all the free learning tools that exist in our gigantic world. You can get free books, watch free videos, and even take free courses all online. The box you use to look up different bits of pointless information can actually be used for something much more meaningful and valuable.

Reflection

Always reflect on yourself in order to make sure you are continually growing. Look inside to see what things might have been bugging you, or how you might have been allowing certain things to affect your life. Ask yourself where there's room for growth and where you might have been focusing too much time and energy.

Reflect on those around you, questioning if they are helping you grow or breaking you down. Reflect on the world and how that is affecting you as well. Are there certain political factors that are causing different emotions? What is happening around you that is helping you learn, and what might be making things even more challenging than they already are.

Do not reflect to the point that it is worried rumination. Reflecting is productive and aims to achieve something you do not have in your waking mind. Rumination involves sitting there and worrying over every last detail about something that you have no control over.

CONCLUSION:

Throughout this book, you've learned a lot of new information, some that is valuable specifically to you, and some that is more general in terms of learning. There might have been a few things you already knew, and maybe there were ideas you never would have thought of on your own. There are a few key takeaways that are the most important parts of understanding this book at its core:

- Everyone learns in a different way, but it's dependent upon how we were raised, the biology we were born with, and the lifestyle in which we live. In our changing world, it's important to make sure we put an emphasis on the future of learning not only for ourselves but for future generations.

- Our memories are very complex, but it all starts with a sensory reaction. From there, we tell our brains to either store it just for a moment or send it through to our long-term memory after it's passed through the prefrontal cortex. There are many bad habits we might partake in that limit our memories, so it's important to know what foods or substances to avoid in order to make sure we promote memory health.

- There are many ways to improve your memory, but the most important part is understanding the things you learn rather than just memorizing information. Your memory is like a garden that needs to be tended to, and you have to remember that if you don't water it, it won't thrive.

- Concentration is all about focusing your brain by tapping into the mechanics and inner workings of your mind. When you are able to finally concentrate, you can reduce study times and improve on the things that you know.

- In order to learn quickly, you have to make sure that you are switching things up and incorporating a wide variety of information and sources into your daily life. Make sure you practice different techniques in order to achieve a level of speedy learning.

- The most important part of growing your mind, accelerating learning, and improving memory is to make sure that you have the right mindset. You can do this by applying both creative and analytic ways of thinking.

OTHER BOOKS BY TRAVIS O'RYAN

Book 1 Description here.

Book 1 Link

Book 2 Description here.

Book 2 Link

Book 3 Description here.

Book 3 Link

DID YOU ENJOY THIS BOOK?

I want to thank you for purchasing and reading this book. I really hope you got a lot out of it.

Can I ask a quick favor though?

If you enjoyed this book I would really appreciate it if you could leave me a positive review on Amazon.

I love getting feedback from my customers and reviews on Amazon really do make a difference. I read all my reviews and would really appreciate your thoughts.

Thanks so much.

Travis O'Ryan

p.s. You can <u>click here</u> to go directly to the book on Amazon and leave your review.

Made in the USA
Middletown, DE
21 November 2019